You Are Worthy

A PERSONAL STORY OF RECOVERY AND HOPE

Lucy Quigley

Lucy Quigley Books
New York, New York

Lucy Quigley Books
New York, New York
www.lucyquigley.com

Book Layout ©2017 BookDesignTemplates.com
Copy editing ©2017 StephanieGunning.com
Cover design ©2017 Lucy Quigley
Photography ©2017 Mia Quigley

Special discounts are available on quantity purchases by schools, associations, and others. For details, contact the publisher.

You Are Worthy/ Lucy Quigley. —1st ed.
ISBN 978-0-692-84632-2

Contents

*For anyone who feels unworthy, insecure, or unsure
about what lies ahead*

Love is forever.
Our life is love.
Love in darkness,
The pain will sever.
Stay strong, and do what is right.
Out from under,
Will emerge a new light.

Preface

According to the Walden Center for Education and Research, 20 percent of college students have or previously had an eating disorder. Only 10 percent of students with a clinical eating disorder will actually receive treatment, according to Mirasol Eating Disorder Recovery Centers. Furthermore, eating disorders are known to have the highest mortality rate of any mental illness.

My name is Lucy and I am one of the one in ten getting treatment. I am nineteen years old and I come from a small town south of Boston, Massachusetts. The reason I am writing this book is to share my personal story of recovery and hope. If you have an eating disorder, I want to let you know that I am okay, and that you also are okay, and to reassure you that we are never alone, not even when we are lost in a situation that feels like a living death. As of this writing, I have been in treatment for one year and I am hopeful about my future.

My name means "light." Saint Lucy (or Lucia), who lived in the Roman Empire, was a bringer of light. Today she is also known as the patron saint for eyes and seeing. Some people have told me that on the outside I "perfectly" fit the meaning of my name. Yet on the inside I often feel surrounded by darkness and as if I've been shattered—broken to pieces.

I may or may not be like you for a number of different reasons. You may be struggling with drinking, cutting, eating, or something else. Our backgrounds may be dissimilar. But in this world we all are similar in some ways and can relate to one another through our ability for empathy.

Right now, I am in the midst of overcoming depression, anxiety, and an eating disorder. For anyone who relates to those aspects of me, by reading my story I want you to know you are not alone like I formerly thought I was. This struggle is common, and some of the brightest, happiest, and most successful people in the world have faced this debilitating challenge at one point in their lives. Fortunately, the challenges that we face do not, and NEVER will, define us, as long as we do not let them. I am learning how I am worth so much more, as are you, no matter the struggle you face.

It is important to know that you are worthy—worthy of love, attention, and happiness. Underlying a lot of the problems young people have is that we do not feel good enough. The pressures in our society pertaining to body image and the associations that we all tie to beauty based on image alone impact us all to an extent. We subconsciously fall under a spell of comparing ourselves to idealized versions of human beings that we see in edited photographs in magazines. It is easy to fall into the trap of believing we are not good enough, to continually put down and shame our bodies and appearances, and even to discount our successes as unworthy compared to those of someone else. Very often what we are looking at is not real, however; it is a FAKE, twisted, filtered, Photoshopped version of reality. Yet we continue to let this diminish us and lessen our feelings of adequacy and worth.

As young people we are striving to identify our real selves and determine where we truly belong. We live in a culture that negatively impacts us and interferes with this process. As a result, chronic self-criticism is a part of many of our lives. I mean, who hasn't at some point in time struggled with food or dieting as a result of trying to look and feel a certain way? Negative self-image is something that affects most of us in some way.

For the purpose of reading my story it does not matter whether or not you have struggled with an eating disorder. Most people, with rare exception, get wrapped up in their own worlds of striving for something they perceive to be better and beating themselves up for falling short of perfection.

We all fall prey to the harmful effects of relentless access to social media and constant messages we see from our exposure to movies, TV, and fashion magazines, imprinting ridiculous standards of beauty in our minds. We are stuck living for an edited Instagram post, forgetting what really exists before our eyes in the present moment. As we strive to recreate these curated versions of reality, we beat ourselves up for not being as cool, beautiful, or successful as celebrities. Is it any wonder that today, the rates of depression and anxiety among young women of college age have never been higher?

Behind the perfectly posed girl standing in front of a gorgeously sparkling sunset is a real person with real shit to contend with, real struggles that are not always as pretty as a picture. Yet regardless, everyone seems to filter out the bad and tries to pretend everything is perfect and beautiful.

Real life cannot be edited. It will never be perfect because life is constantly changing. Imperfectness is what makes our world TRULY beautiful.

Lately I am learning how our worthiness should never be tied to our outer appearances. The impact we leave behind us wherever we go in life is what matters, not how much we weigh or what size pants we wear, or how many likes we get for our social media posts. For crying out loud, do you think President Barack Obama or Martin Luther King, Jr., will be remembered for how much they weighed? HECK NO! The greatest leaders in our history are remembered for the real actions they took. The meaningful legacy we will leave behind for future generations will come from our inner beauty and the efforts we make to better ourselves and the world around us in whatever way we can during our lives. As young people we have the potential to do incredible things in the years to come.

In this book I am not going to provide a narrative of triumph, a magical happily ever after, or describe the one special antidote I have obtained in order to fight depression, anxiety, and eating disorders. I am still learning about myself and how to respond to my illness each and every day. Like everybody else, I am in the thick of things. Unfortunately, for the majority of people in my situation there never will be a single quick fix. Recovery is a process.

I am here to offer you some insights from my journey, and give you hope. I want to be a voice representing the internal feelings that millions of other college-age girls, mothers, athletes, and even men and boys—people of all shapes and sizes—have when they are impacted by an eating disorder. And I would like to reassure you that you are not alone—to let you know that even in the midst of our problems we all have the power inside us to change our situation for the better.

CHAPTER ONE

Never Good Enough

"Courage can be contagious and hope can take on a life of its own."

—Michelle Obama

I am not particularly special, nor have I ever considered myself to be special. Yes, I did well in high school and got accepted to a good college as a result, but I have grown up feeling undeserving and unworthy of being good enough to pursue my passions. My whole life I have struggled from a lack of confidence

I have struggled with wondering where in the world I belong. I have never felt that I was interested primarily in one thing, which made it hard for me to feel accepted. In school, I always loved music, but I also loved sports. I loved acting and performing in plays at the local community theater. I loved doing math and science, but I also loved psychology, history, language, writing, and reading literature. I could never choose just one thing, be just one thing, or fit into one category no matter how much I tried or wanted to.

I also never had one solid group of friends. I felt like I floated between different groups of people and although I could get along with pretty much anyone, I still felt alone in myself and isolated. I wondered why I could relate to so many different kinds of people yet not find a group to belong in. I could never be sporty enough to be just the sporty girl. I didn't consider myself musical or talented enough to be just the music or drama girl. I couldn't be outgoing enough to be the party girl. I felt I was not smart enough to be with the kids who read at lunch or debated heated political subjects for hours on end. I felt stuck in the absolute middle of the whirlwind of life and never felt there was a place for me.

By looking at me from the outside, I am sure that friends, family, and loved ones never would have guessed I had been feeling any of that. Currently I am attending New York University. I have been blessed with an amazing family. I am the oldest of four kids, two boys and two girls. In high school although my life may have seemed a "perfect" picture to onlookers, by junior year on the inside I had begun falling to pieces.

I was voted friendliest in my high school class. I was captain of our school's varsity swim team. I was the concert master of the orchestra. I made high honor roll every semester. I was a violin teacher, as well as a swimming coach and lifeguard. I drove around in a little pink Volkswagen Beetle with a smile on my face and my white fluffy dog sitting in the front seat. So yes, I can see why I must have seemed to have everything going for me.

While I was capable of doing those things, on the inside I was struggling with a debilitating amount of lack of confidence, never feeling worthy. I had a tendency to isolate myself because of my lack of confidence. I therefore never attended many parties in high school and I was lonely.

Drinking isn't for everyone. We all have personal associations with it from experiences with alcohol that may or may not contribute to a choice for engagement. For me, I didn't like that drinking made me feel out of control. And having seen the repercussions of substance abuse, the thought of drinking frightened me. I felt I was not cool enough, and would not fit in well with my friends at their parties if I wasn't drinking. So it was ironic and unfortunate for me that I got busted by the cops the very first time I went to a big high school party. This happened after only being there for fifteen minutes and not even having consumed any alcohol.

Because I was always taught to be honorable, I didn't run when the other kids did and I consequently got my name taken down by the police. The cops did not care that I had not been drinking. As punishment for being underage at a party with open alcohol, I was cited as ineligible for the National Honor Society. I was suspended from participating in the sports and music programs at school, and I was also forced to be evaluated by a psychologist who specialized in drug and alcohol abuse. All for "being in the presence" of alcohol once.

For a girl who had never gone to a high school party let alone had taken a sip of alcohol in her entire life, this experience was a traumatizing and humiliating one to say the very least. I lost all confidence in myself after that, and thought less and less of myself. My entire grade heard the story and I was embarrassed, believing everyone now saw me as the "dork" at the party who didn't know to run from the cops.

And I was angry. I felt discriminated against, in a sense, because I saw plenty of other kids who lied their way out of the incident, cheated, and partied with alcohol every weekend and still got to be part of the National Honor Society, which I had always been one of my achievement goals. I thought to myself, *Wow those kids really can do it all flawlessly, good for them. I must be a failure in every way. Now I can't fit into NHS because I'm an idiot who doesn't know how to run from cops, and not 'bad ass' or cool enough like those kids.*

Frankly, I lost my understanding of what it meant to be honorable. The rules didn't make sense to me anymore, and since I was always trying to follow the rules it was confusing.

This incident ruined my senior year for me. I became WAY too scared after the incident ever to try smoking or drinking, which gave me a reason to keep to myself. To be quite honest, I sort of preferred to have the time alone to think and reflect. People would call me very independent, and I would agree. Because I am a hard worker and don't like wasting time and energy on things I feel are unnecessary, being alone suited me.

I am pretty introspective, a very good listener, and have a high degree of sensitivity to others and their feelings. I am the type of person with whom others share things. All sorts of different people will open up to me and tell me their deepest secretes and most intimate stories. But while they gravitate toward me to tell me about themselves, one of my struggles always has been finding my own voice. I wasn't sharing my stories until now because I couldn't answer the questions: Where do I belong? And who will be there for me when I need someone?

At times we can get caught up in being there for others at the expense of our own needs. We may end up neglecting ourselves and our own self-care if we don't feel worthy enough to put ourselves first. That is where many things for me started going wrong. But I'm realizing now that I can allow myself to accept who I am for all that I am, and this made me ready to share my story.

During my freshman year of college, my repressed feelings of sadness, anger, loneliness, shame, and lack of confidence were triggered more and more, and they got progressively more out of my control. I struggled with chronic depression and anxiety, and then was hospitalized during the following summer to treat symptoms of an eating disorder.

The transition from living at home with our parents to attending college and living in a dorm among other students is tough for a lot of people. I understand now that this transition often will spark depression, increased anxiety, and eating disorders, as it did for me. The uncertainty of finding ourselves, deciding what we want to do in our lives and where we are going to belong in the world can make us feel incredibly vulnerable. We no longer really belong at home, and at the same time our feet are only halfway through the door of the "new world." To successfully launch our lives, we essentially have to rebuild ourselves, form our own identities, reexamine what we know, and decide what we want to be, all from scratch. Everything seems so unknown.

I want to spend time in this book explaining the feelings that someone endures under these circumstances, as well as provide you with some information and insight into depression, anxiety, and eating disorders, and why they happen.

As I undertake this task, I am aware that you could be thinking I am by no means a "perfect" or "good enough" role model for everyone who has an eating disorder to follow. When I set out to write this book, I felt this way myself.

However, I have since realized that it does not matter how I compare to anyone else. Each of us has our own story, and we are entitled to have it. Being a perfect example of healing is an unattainable goal. Perfection simply is not real And anyhow, our imperfections make us interesting and ultimately make life beautiful.

I am just one girl with one story. But hopefully you will agree that our similarities outweigh our differences. Currently, I am still working each and every day on getting better, on my recovery. I hope telling you my story will help you find a little bit of hope, encouragement, and strength to fight through your own moments of darkness and strive to better yourself and achieve a greater purpose in your life.

We learn from each other's struggles. Through our differences we can learn to come together, with empathy, as one. We all are different and we all have different stories. Because of these differences we can learn from each other. Please use my resources to help develop your own.

If I am able to inspire you in even the smallest way to realize the strength, power, and resilience that is within you, I will be satisfied that I have done what I set out to do in this book. My goal is for you to see the power and light held within you, to realize your dreams, and to use your own power to become the best person that you ALLREADY are despite any challenges and setbacks you experience. Knowing that YOU have the power to make your life what YOU want it to be, I hope I can give you courage to fight through what sometimes seems to be infinite pain and interminable darkness.

CHAPTER TWO

What Is an Eating Disorder?

"It may be necessary to encounter the defeats so you can know who you are."

—Maya Angelou

A n eating disorder is a severe mental illness, one that has the highest mortality rate of any other mental disorder. However, when some people hear the phrase *mental illness* the first thing that comes to their minds is that sufferers are psychos, crazies, weirdos, outcasts, serial killers, or people who have lost their minds and are therefore incapable of functioning in society.

It is time to remove this stigma and bring attention to the fact that some of the highest functioning, most successful people in the world have to struggle constantly to find their way through the darkness and pain of a mental illness.

Having a mental illness does NOT mean you are any of those things I said above. It does NOT define your worthiness or lovability. Furthermore, mental illnesses really should be talked about NO differently than any other types of sickness or physical injury.

Mental illnesses, such as chronic anxiety, depression, and eating disorders, all continue to have certain unexplainable stigmas and stereotypes associated with them that make everyone seem to have a "hush hush" attitude toward them. With the prevalence and seriousness of these conditions, why on earth does this continue to be the case?

Mental illnesses can be incredibly difficult to wrap your mind around. It's hard to understand what they are and why they happen. And for those who have never battled with a mental illness, it is nearly impossible to understand what is happening within someone who is enduring such a struggle. Due to this difficulty, most people really don't know how to react or comprehend these problems, and often people are unwilling to take the time to figure out what treatment for these challenging issues entails. Most people have a much easier time accepting and understanding a physical injury.

When someone has a broken leg, it is easy to drop off a get-well-soon package or simply ask someone how her leg is feeling. It doesn't seem fair that with someone suffering from depression or anxiety, no one knows how to ask or how to act. The two injuries are equally debilitating in different ways.

The main difference between a broken leg and an eating disorder is the emotional component. With emotional injuries we have to internally fix an injured heart and soul. This is more complicated and occurs at a deeper place inside us than healing from a physical injury.

Yet does that mean eating disorders should go undiscussed in our day-to-day lives, and continue to be swept under the table? Should we pretend they are nonexistent? ABSOLUTELY NOT! In my opinion these things should be discussed more, because they are that much MORE complicated. There is so much MORE to learn. And the more we can be there for EACH OTHER, the better off all of us will be.

Our tendency of not wanting to be there for others or to hear about people's struggles, or pretending that our own do not exist, is a cultural phenomenon that needs to be recognized and changed, in my opinion.

When you say to someone, "Oh yeah, and by the way, I've been struggling with an eating disorder and have been severely anxious and depressed," chances are they won't know what to say in response. Very understandably, it can be hard for others to relate to or sympathize with your eating disorder. This is true because, as I said before, it is nearly impossible to know what we are feeling if you have not felt it yourself. But as someone who has dealt with this type of emotional pain and is currently still dealing with this pain, one thing I have learned is that even if people cannot understand, allowing people to remain in your company is essential.

We need love in order to live. Therefore missing out on events in order to fulfill the "needs" of your eating disorder interferes with an important aspect of life. Hiding out is not real living. To clarify this statement, I used to often say no to the invitations of friends (even cute boys) who would ask me to go get an ice cream or have dinner with them. This was because of my eating disorder. I felt afraid of getting fat from having a scoop of ice cream or a slice of pizza.

I know, it sounds totally crazy, but to me, when I was in my darkest state, missing out on real life fun was totally worth it if it meant I could be skinny. As a result of saying no, no, no all the time to everyone, however, I found myself in a dark world of lonesome social isolation. Living in isolation I have learned from personal experience IS NOT good living.

Eating disorders lead to a bizarre stagnation of time in the period when we are immersed in darkness and pain. Because we shut out the world while we are young, we are missing out on important social experiences and normal developmental milestones that include peer interaction, the building of relationships, finding our real voices, and being connected to society and our world. Eating disorders are a way of numbing our inner pain and avoiding the instability of change that accompanies life transitions. Essentially, our behavior when we have eating disorders prevents us from facing the world successfully and growing up.

My greatest fear in telling people about my eating disorder is that they will think differently about me, perhaps seeing me as a "charity case" or perceiving me as debilitated in some way. Yes, while my disorder, in a way does debilitate me at times and it has kept me from functioning appropriately in many different circumstances and situations, I am still, and always will remain the same me. There is just a sad and frightened, vulnerable little part inside me that you might not have known was there before I told you. If anything, I have now come to learn more about who I really am because of facing the challenges I have faced.

One of the most challenging aspects of recovering from an eating disorder is that food is a necessity for survival.

Disorders related to food are actually quite similar to other substance abuse disorders. The main difference between them is that food is the chosen substance of abuse, whether that means overeating, under eating, or a combination of binging on food and purging food by forcing yourself to throw up. There have been studies done suggesting that sugar is as addictive as cocaine. But if you were addicted to cocaine, you could stop using it and live, whereas you can never stop eating and survive. You can give up cigarettes, but you can't give up food. Essentially, the point is that you cannot survive without food, which makes it much more difficult to undergo a successful recovery. We are abusing the food we eat to numb the pain of very complicated and deep underlying issues.

Those who struggle from binge eating cannot just become "sober" from food. You cannot stop eating in the same manner that alcoholics can stop drinking.

Those who struggle with anorexia have to give themselves permission to go against everything their minds are telling them in a given moment. They need to see past the false mental blockages they have created around food and eating. Nothing is more difficult.

Those with bulimia need to practice moderation. They also need to learn to sit with the uncomfortable feelings that fullness brings them.

Food will always be in front of us, which is why recovery can be so difficult for those of us with eating disorders. If you have one, you have to adopt completely new values and develop an understanding of holistic health, nourishment, and moderation.

If someone you know suffers from an eating disorder, please encourage them to get treatment and stand by them. For additional ideas, please see the Resources section at the back of the book. If you are suffering, please find the courage to help yourself. Take the first step by telling someone and asking for support.

Remember, through challenges such as these, we all have the power to change our circumstances, but we must be willing to fight harder than we ever have fought for anything else. I promise you that this fight is a fight that's worth it. Living through an eating disorder is not good living. It is hell. It is a stagnated time where you are throwing away your potential and moments of your real life that you can never, ever get back. You cannot live entrapped within pain and darkness. Live for more. Live for your true self.

I have found that when it comes to mental illnesses, such as depression, anxiety, or eating disorders, people tend not to want to ask questions. At the same time, I know that people also do not want it to seem like they don't care about us. There is a tough line to walk, because there definitely is a fine line between trying to be supportive and coming off as overbearing. At times, the way people ask questions or try to show their support can actually come across as the complete opposite of being supportive. However, I will say that for anyone who knows someone going through a struggle, PLEASE KNOW that in appropriate circumstances you SHOULD ask!

I know personally that I am very open and honest, and I understand that not everyone is, but I happen to gain a tremendous amount of comfort knowing someone cares when they simply ask me genuinely how I am doing. Having someone simply ask is way better then feeling alone and consumed by your struggles.

We need to be present and available for each other.

Additionally, what many people do not realize about eating disorders is that they are symptomatic of other root issues. They manifest in people's lives when something else is a problem and has not been addressed. No one just wakes up one morning and decides to be anorexic, just like how no one would wake up and think, *Hmm, I'm going to break my leg today.* There is always a cause for a broken bone, just as there is always a cause for an eating disorder.

Because there is always something way more going on I want to emphasize again how it is never your fault when you are struggling with an eating disorder yourself. You need to stop the self-blame and chronic self-hatred, and realize that no one would ever ask for this to happen.

The root of an eating disorder is an incredibly complicated and individualized matter that differs for each and every person who faces one. For example, the root cause could be a trauma, instilled ideas, or abuse. Depression and anxiety get tangled in with these issues as well, and sometimes those can be genetically caused problems, even though there also are usually deeper and more specific triggers that planted seeds for depression and anxiety to grow.

Although some people are more susceptible to developing depression and anxiety, nobody just wakes up and has depression. It has causes. Nature and nurture, from what I have learned, both play roles in them. Interactions with the environment we are in impact us all tremendously, whether or not we realize it.

Overall, I have struggled immensely with self-acceptance. I have never been okay with feeling like I am not one defined thing. I have never seen myself as beautiful, so I have never been able to accept myself and my body as good enough. I strive for perfection, and have trouble settling with anything less. I am unsure of my future therefore I struggled immensely with the transition of leaving home and going to college. I have trouble letting go of anything. My sensitivity toward others and the circumstances and changes going on around me affects me tremendously. I seem to absorb everything that's happening around me. Then I bottle up my feelings. I don't always know how to express them in a healthy way.

For me my need to express all of these repressed emotions manifested as an eating disorder. This may not make total sense to you now, but I will explain throughout this book in more detail why eating disorders grow, develop, and turn into an overpowering and abusive inner voice that seems impossible to escape from.

In fifth grade, when I was only ten years old, I can remember telling myself how fat and ugly I was compared to my friends. I looked at my younger sister as if she was a tall, slender, stunning super model. I saw everyone and everything around me in this beautiful light, yet I could not look at myself in the mirror and ever think the same way.

I went through middle school and high school constantly coping with these insecurities and constantly in an internal fight with an evil inner bully that was continuously convincing me that I was never good enough for anyone or anything.

Like many high school students, I thought I knew what I wanted and who I wanted to be when I grew up. I was dead set on attending New York University to study the music business and one day work in the music industry. I applied early decision, sent in audition tapes, got accepted into the program, and was on cloud nine. I thought this was it! I would go to NYU and my life would be set. I thought that everything had finally culminated and come together for me. Little did I know that I had a bumpy road ahead of me.

I also went to NYU with an overly romanticized vision of what New York City would be like in my mind. One of my downfalls, but also one of my greatest attributes, is my ability to dream. As a dreamer, I dream of infinite possibilities and ideas for the future. I believe in magic. Before I got to school, was seeking a love that was so consuming that not even life itself can break it. I pictured myself rocking the subways, shopping on Fifth Avenue, getting free passes to concerts, ice skating in Rockefeller Center with my Prince Charming, and living it up every way possible in the "greatest city in the world." What I thought would be the greatest place for me to be turned out to probably be the worst at the time.

This is okay now. Today I have accepted my circumstances and situation for how it is. If it weren't for the experiences I went through my freshman year, I would not have had the chance to grow into a stronger version of myself. Nor would I have realized the importance of being open minded not only toward other people, but toward the real me.

As mentioned earlier, I never had much self-confidence, even though on the outside, through my mini successes, it may have seemed to other people as if I did. When I first arrived at NYU I was excited for my classes to begin and to start pursuing my major, but also very nervous. As the year progressed, these parts of my life all sort of started getting out of my control. I thought music business was all I ever wanted. I was all in. But as I looked at all the smart people around me, I convinced myself I was worthless.

I was consumed with school work and signed up for eight classes in my second semester, which was a very heavy course load. I felt like a fake, a total phony. On the outside I was gung ho for the music business, but internally I felt like a failure and as if I was lying to myself and the world. Deep down I knew this was not what I wanted. I knew I could never be happy in an industry that pays artists fractions of cents per sale for the streaming use of songs that they create. I also could not come to terms with being in an industry that discriminates against women. But most of all, I genuinely felt that I did not belong, that I was not cool enough, smart enough, or talented enough to be in a program of the caliber of the one at NYU. I did not fit in, and felt completely alone.

I struggled immensely with the process of making new friends my freshman year. At a school as big as NYU, it is very easy to slip into yourself and become anonymous. Coming from a tiny high school in Massachusetts, I thought I wanted this change. I thought I wanted to be an adult living in the city with no real campus. For some reason, I had always pictured college being that way. While I am very independent, however, this kind of college experience was too much for me as a freshman. I absolutely despised the loneliness of it.

My happiness, joy, and admiration for life were slowly slipping away from me. I went out less and less, and became increasingly unhappy with myself. I could not accept the fact that what I had thought I wanted turned out to not be the case. But I also believed I couldn't let myself or others down. I was terrified of being seen as a "failure." I knew deep down that something needed to change because everything started to spiral more and more out of my control. I felt like an outcast in my own dorm room and did not feel safe going back to my room at night. I felt judged, left out, hurt, and humiliated by those around me.

Throughout my freshman year, I kept thinking the situation was completely my fault and that I deserved to feel as bad as I did. I told myself that I was the problem. I kept bullying myself by saying over and over again that there was something severely wrong with me. I saw myself as nothing and underserving of anything good. My depression and anxiety continued to grow from week to week. I decided I was a failure.

In the end, I was a failure who needed a coping mechanism, and this mechanism became my eating disorder.

CHAPTER THREE

Beginning of a New Journey

"Look at how a single candle can both defy and define the darkness."

—Anne Frank

When people ask me about the origin of my eating disorder I have a hard time describing it, for one thing, because I continually find it is nearly impossible for anyone who has not struggled with this kind of disease to fully understand how it happens. And for another thing, because I have trouble understanding it myself.

My relationship with food is a gray area. I don't like naming what I have, as I hate how much labels come to define people and their worth. It is incredibly difficult for me to claim to have an eating disorder because this makes everything that I have been through seem frighteningly real. Saying it aloud is terrifying.

If I were to apply a name to what I have experienced, I would say that I was anorexic for a time. I then became bulimic, and also struggled with binge eating. Now, I am in the midst of learning to fight my disordered thoughts about eating and learn how to fight and recognize when the eating disorder is speaking and not the real me.

At first, I felt so alienated at school that I even convinced myself that I was an outcast among people with eating disorders. I believed it was a problem that my behavior did not fit the bill or belong exclusively to one category. I have since realized how wrong that mentality and mindset is. Just like anything else in life, NOTHING is black and white.

Actually, the majority of people with eating disorders are engaging in more than one disordered behavior to an extent. So when I share my story with others now, as I do when I go to support groups, and sometimes when I am speaking with old friend I haven't seen in a while, I usually just leave it at "I have been struggling with some eating issues."

If you struggle, or anyone you know struggles, with eating issues, know that nobody is ever the same. We are affected differently by our urges. You can never tell by looking at people whether or not they have an eating disorder. People who are affected by this life-debilitating storm of sadness may be overweight, underweight, or average weight.

It is very common for eating disorders to come and go, and to transfer between the different forms. By going to group therapy sessions and seeing other people and hearing their stories I have realized this, and realized how normal and okay it is that I am the way I am. My point is this: Obsession with food, regardless of how that presents itself, is a result of feeling out of control in some other area of your life.

Now I want to describe in a bit more detail what each of these issues has entailed for me. I hope those who have struggled with eating issues will identify with at least a part of what I describe because, as you shall see in my story, I have personally experienced pieces of each of the disorders that are discussed in the next few chapters.

CHAPTER FOUR

Anorexia

"Hear 'anorexia' and you think bone-thin young women—scary-skinny runway models with emaciated figures. But an overlooked group of young people are also struggling with anorexia nervosa: overweight and even obese kids."

—Melissa Dahl

Because I had never been satisfied with who I was, I used to think that by losing weight I would learn how to love myself and finally come to embrace my "inner Beyoncé," or something along those lines. I thought I could achieve perfection through weight loss. I believed if I could just make myself skinnier then everything would be better. I would have more friends, more boys would notice me, I would feel more confident.

For many people, this type of thinking is how eating disorders begin. The fixation with body image and food results from feeling out of control in other areas of life.

At first as I lost weight I thought I was becoming healthier. My intentions were to be healthy and my weight loss was occurring in a somewhat healthful way. But soon losing weight turned into an unbreakable obsession. Gradually I became so carried away with the idea of losing weight that eventually I completely lost control.

I started counting my calories to lose weight in October 2015 and soon I reached a normal weight for my height. By December and January, as I became more and more dissatisfied with my life, my eating habits spiraled out of control.

My food habits paralleled what was going on in my life. The weight loss was never good enough for me, just as I was never "good enough" for my school program, so I kept feeling the "need" to lose more and began eating less and less.

By April 2016, I got to the point where I was eating only 300–500 calories per day. My obsession with avoiding calories became so out of hand that I refused even to chew gum out of my irrational fear of gaining weight from the extra calories and few grams of sugar that are in each piece. I lost close to fifty pounds when I was at my absolute worst.

If you knew me, you would know that fifty pounds was an absurd amount of weight for my body to lose. As a result of what I was doing, I barely had enough energy to make it through each and every day.

During these months I did not go out and I isolated myself from everyone who loved me. I missed out on family gatherings, trips, and social outings with friends. I lost interest in everything I truly loved and cared about: music, swimming, nature, film, culture, friends, family, and loved ones. But in my mind, I decided it was all worth it if it meant being skinny. If friends and family who were around me after my freshman year of college, had not eventually expressed their concerns, this would have continued to escalate. I probably would have been in a very different place then I am right now.

If you see someone you know suddenly dropping weight dramatically like I did, I would advise you to approach them cautiously, sympathetically, and with a high degree of sensitivity to express your concerns. If no one had addressed this weight loss with me and left me alone within myself and my own head, I may not have been able to be here experiencing this journey and now gaining the gift and opportunity of sharing my story.

My mother and father saved my life. Words are inadequate to express the infinite amount of love and appreciation I have for them both for saving my life by intervening when they saw me dramatically dropping weight. Even though I knew I had a problem, I could not have escaped the vicious cycle I was in without help.

Do not try forcing the person you are concerned about to eat, because that simply won't work and comes off as incredibly intrusive. Do not constantly ask this person what she is eating. Believe me, food is on her mind enough as it is. Just be there for her and do not let her be alone—even if this is what she is insisting you do—as loneliness is toxic.

When the time and context seem appropriate, because the person you are hoping to help seems receptive and calm, recommend to her that she seek some sort of help.

By helping someone find a therapist to speak with you truly are saving a life. No exaggeration. Do not forget this. Also do not forget to have empathy for the person with the eating disorder. Changing her mindset is not your job, it is hers. And it is an excruciating task that will take time.

If you have not had an eating disorder yourself, you have to understand that it literally controls every aspect of you, your mind, and your life. I had an amazing therapist explain to me how essentially I was in an abusive relationship with myself. In this scenario, no matter what others are saying to you, you cannot break away from the relationship due to the twisted sense of comfort you have when you're in it. Know that the eating disorder is the one thing we believe we have control over, and we are using it as a way to comfort ourselves when everything else feels out of our control.

CHAPTER FIVE

Bulimia

"We've all got both light and dark inside us.
What matters is the part we choose to act on.
That's who we really are."

—J.K. Rowling

In addition to my rigid and severe caloric restriction, I became compulsively obsessed with running. I counted absolutely every calorie I ate and was compelled to burn at least that same amount by running.

The flip side of compulsive exercise was that sports always had been a positive part of my life. Running gave me a massive release from stress and anxiety over exams in college. I felt so good after a long run that I wanted to just keep going. It gave me an escape from my heightened anxiety, irrational fears, and growing depression. But with the malnourishment that my body was enduring simultaneously, adding running to the equation became a recipe for disaster.

While many people associate bulimia with vomiting, it actually includes a multitude of "purging" type activities, such as long periods of restriction after eating and over exercising to compensate, as well as self-induced vomiting.

After a period of time, my body felt so deprived that I would uncontrollably shove food into my face whenever the situation presented itself. My body was in extreme survival mode. No matter how much I did not want to eat, I could not stop because of the severe deprivation that had preceded it.

Deprivation of any kind will always lead to binging. This does not apply just to food, but this happened for me with food, and I'm going to warn you now, it was not pretty.

Binging felt as if some other alter ego had taken over my body. I had zero control of myself and my actions. I could not stop eating no matter how much I wanted to. I would become so full that I could feel the food coming back up my stomach and throat. I could not deal with either the physical or emotional feelings, or with the inescapable guilt.

That is when I started purging in numerous ways to compensate after the times I uncontrollably ate. In the moment, purging gave me temporary relief and made me feel in control of the "mistakes" I had made. The purging, however, escalated as well, and my view of what overeating was and what regular eating was became more and more distorted. Ultimately the purging made me feel worse—even more ashamed of myself and what I saw myself turning into.

My depression grew. I could not recognize the girl looking back at me in the mirror. She was a miserable, lonely, hopeless person who saw herself as ugly no matter what anyone said or did.

In case you are unaware, making yourself throw up actually cannot reverse what you have just eaten or consumed. On average, only 50 percent of what you consume can be eliminated, and most of the nutrients, sugars, and fats will have already started the process of being stored and filtered throughout your system. Compensating for overeating by purging is more mental than actually effective.

While anorexia may be the leading cause of death by eating disorder, the dangers that come with bulimia are irreversible. A few of the many consequences of bulimia include heart problems, dental problems, and reproductive issues. There also are severe physical injuries that come due to the lack of nourishment in combination with excessive exercising. For example, stress fractures are incredibly common for people with eating disorders because our bones become weakened. Even so we continue to beat our bodies up over and over.

I recently had a near stress fracture of my right foot from over exercising. Luckily my foot turned out not to be broken. But I did have to wear a boot and spent two weeks hobbling around New York City looking like an absolute lunatic.

Please be honest with yourself, and take control before you lose things that you can never get back. We are only given one body. Own it, embrace it, and care for it in the best way possible.

I have had discussions with people in which they said to me, "I just don't understand how anyone could ever make themselves throw up; that is just disgusting." They were not trying to be cruel. They did not know I was experiencing an eating disorder.

Believe me I am beyond ashamed of my actions and am well aware of how disgusting and harmful vomiting is to my body. The thing to remember is that no one plans on forcing herself to vomit. No one plans on starving her body to a state of severe deprivation and malnourishment, and then having to binge eat uncontrollably in order to survive. No one intentionally does these things "for fun."

Someone else also unknowingly said to me, "You look so great. I tried to be anorexic once to lose weight, but literally couldn't do it. Hahaha. I just love food too much." There is a myth that anorexia is a choice.

Remember: No one who is anorexic chooses to be. Who in her right mind would ever want to hurt herself like that?

By May of my freshman year, as finals were rolling around, my anxiety was mounting. My eating habits were a mess and my control over food continued to be my coping mechanism for my depression, anxiety, and feelings of inadequacy. My weight loss continued and I obsessively stepped on the scale multiple times every day. My weight had diminished each time I looked. I was withering away.

My overall anxiety continued to increase along with the decrease in my weight. I can remember having severe panic attacks before going to my microeconomics class, for example. My heart pulsed uncontrollably, my hands were shaking, and I felt like I was going to die.

For anyone who has struggled with anxiety, you can understand that when a panic attack like this hits you, nothing else in the world can be seen for what it actually is. Everything is distorted, and you feel as if you have lost control of your entire body.

I just have to get through these exams, I told myself, *and then I can go home for the summer and everything will be fine.*

Little did I know that everything would be far from fine. These things do not just magically disappear by a change of location. Yes, location and environment have a huge impact on us, and can be a temporary solution for anxiety that triggers us, but they are by no means a cure to our problems.

CHAPTER SIX

Binge Eating Disorder

*"No matter what we weigh, those of us who are
compulsive eaters have anorexia of the soul. We refuse
to take in what sustains us. We live lives of deprivation.
And when we can't stand it any longer, we binge."*

—Geneen Roth

As time progressed, my binge eating got more and more out of control. The difference between bulimia and binge eating is that binge eaters do not compensate for overeating, yet they feel incredible shame, guilt, disgust, depression, and self-loathing after a binge.

I got to a point where I was so exhausted I no longer had the fight in me to purge. I was so depressed I did not care about anything anymore except food. By the end of the summer I had gained back more than half the weight I had lost and felt even worse about myself then before. While anorexia and bulimia are incredibly dangerous, those of us with eating disorders have more comfort when engaging in those two behaviors than in binge eating because anorexia and bulimia give us the illusion of control. Really it is not we "ourselves" who are in control, because it is not our real selves in control but the voice of the damned eating disorder, which sounds like the voice of a devil within you. The eating disorder is taking over and speaking in place of the real you, which is now buried and lost within the eating disorder.

One of the most important steps we take in recovery from binge eating disorder, anorexia, and bulimia is learning to discern the voice of our eating disorder, which is mean spirited and critical, from our real inner voice, which is loving and compassionate. Making this distinction helps us come out of our enmeshed web of fog and confusion. Of course, this takes practice, time, patience, therapy, and the willingness to take a huge risk of learning to trust your real self and your real body while everything in your head is telling you the opposite.

While the binge eating feels out of control, and emotionally can be so taxing, you have to realize that the voice forcing you to binge is the same voice that is forcing you to restrict eating and purge. This eating disorder, no matter how it shows up, is overpowering the real you. Whatever way it shows up in a given moment, it is threatening and dangerous.

Eating disorders are dangerous because we can begin to perceive them as us. We have to learn to separate our real selves from any illusions within our minds. All types of eating disorders are harmful and detract from being who we really are. While we may feel better through restriction, the problems we really have to deal with do not just disappear through this method of control.

CHAPTER SEVEN

The Not-so-Sexy Lifeguard

"Even the model's we see in magazines wish they could look like their own images."

—Cheri K. Erdman

I had convinced myself that finishing off my year at NYU and returning home for the summer would magically make everything okay and make the anxiety, depression, and disordered eating patterns that I had developed at school go away. I did not know what was in store for me in the fall, only that for the time being returning home would make everything better—at least for a little while.

I started my lifeguarding job and was able to cover up my problems with food for a while. I distracted myself from my feelings of inadequacy and anxiety through the joy I got from being around children and giving them swim lessons, and seeing the familiar faces of friends and family from home. But this did not change what was going on deep within me.

As the summer progressed and the prospect of returning to school in the fall approached slowly, my anxiety climbed, and my fear and depression about the unknown world back at school manifested itself more and more. Everything in the future was so unknown that I felt utterly confused and unsure of everything lying ahead of me. I had no idea what to do. The one thing I did know, however, was that I could not go back to studying the music business. All I could do was take each day one at a time, and try to enjoy the happy moments of my summer school break while I could.

One of the hardest things for me throughout the process of healing from an eating disorder has been people's encourage-ment and fascination with my weight loss. Why does society in general continue to value thinness as such an ideal and see it as an amazing and worthy accomplishment? This core idea has been very detrimental to my health!

By looking at me, maybe you would not think I have been battling self-destructing demons. So if you can take only one thing from this book, remember that. You literally can NEVER actually know what is going on inside someone, even if they make a "perfect" picture on the outside. You never truly can see what happens behind closed doors.

The comments about my body were heightened because of being a lifeguard. I spent 80 percent of my days wearing a swimsuit in front of people who had known me my entire life. The pool I worked at was like a second home to me, and the people who know me there were like family and had watched me grow up. People therefore said misguided things to me like, "Oh my goodness you have never looked better" or "What's your secret, what can I do to look like that?" Or "I am so happy for you. You must be doing great at school because you look fantastic."

I know everyone's intention in making comments such as these came from a place of love. However, little did anyone know I was coming out of the hardest year of my life and had never felt as unhappy as I did then. As a result of comments like these, I continued to feel like something was severely wrong with me because everyone around me was cheering me on for what I had just done to my body.

No one knew how much pain I actually was in.

CHAPTER EIGHT

The Breaking Point

"In the midst of tears, I found there was, within me,
an invincible calm. I realized that throughout it all,
that . . . in the midst of winter, I found there was,
within me, an invincible summer."

—Albert Camus

O n the morning of July 10, I reached a breaking point. I woke up in a cold sweat and could feel my anxiety climbing. My mom, brother, and sister had left for a community service trip to the Appalachian Mountains. I was at home with my other younger brother and my dad. I was lonely and feeling left behind.

I think the uncertainty of having most of my family away triggered that specific anxiety attack, but the anxiety also had been building up continuously throughout my entire first year at college, and as I have mentioned before, repressing emotions and feelings is something I do when I feel out of control. Those feelings were ready to erupt. I have since learned that suppression causes internal anxiety that will continually to build in intensity until eventually it takes you over.

I felt the panic attack start to consume me. I could not function, but did not know what to do. So what did I do? Eat. And not just eat, I freaking chowed down on everything that was in my vicinity.

I cannot remember exactly what I ate, but I think it was something like six bowls of Cinnamon Toast Crunch® cereal; three peanut butter and banana sandwiches; a bacon, egg, and cheese on a bagel; two granola bars; a banana pancake; an English muffin; a pint of Ben and Jerry's® Cookie Dough ice cream; an iced latte with whole milk; and then whatever was left of a gallon of vanilla ice cream that was in the freezer; and then cereal again, until the box was empty. I swear on my dog's life that I am not exaggerating one bit.

Now, after reading that list, you probably think I am a full-blown psycho. Maybe, if I was Michael Phelps, that would have been an okay binge, but for my much smaller body that was a complete overdose of toxic abuse. I felt sick, but I could not stop eating no matter how much I wanted to. I ate nonstop for probably close to two hours. My stomach was in such excruciating pain afterward that I could barely move.

There is actual scientific evidence that explains why a binge happens and why people use food as a coping mechanism for anxiety. You see, in moments of high stress, due to evolutionary reasons, it is our natural instinct to turn to food for comfort and safety. When we eat food, one of our neurotransmitters, *dopamine,* is released in the brain. This comforts us and makes us feel temporarily better.

Although I was full beyond my body's capacity, I could not stop eating because I was in so much emotional pain. I was using the food to medicate myself with the feel good hormones my brain released as a result of eating these "comfort" foods. Of course when I could eat no longer on that day, I felt even worse off than I did before I started eating.

So what did I do to compensate then? Compulsively, I locked myself in the bathroom and forced myself to throw up until every last bit of food I had eaten exited my body. Of course, now I know this is physically impossible to do. At the time, I did not care. I spent four and a half hours that day in July locked in that bathroom making myself throw up as much as I could. No one knew except me.

Physically, I felt terrible. I was tired. I was dizzy. The room was spinning from all the throwing up. My stomach was in pain. My body was energetically depleted. My throat burned from the exorbitant amount of bile that was exiting my body. My knuckles were dripping with blood from my teeth hitting the same spot on my hand over and over again for hours as I stuck my hand down my throat to initiate the gag sensation that enabled me to vomit. I was depressed and wanted to die. This day was when I realized I had to stop.

I knew my problem was out of my control. Not only was I in bad physical condition, but emotionally I was a wreck too. I had suicidal thoughts and even started writing farewell letters to the people I loved.

In short, I knew I needed help. I knew I could no longer fix this on my own.

I somehow found courage for the first time in that moment to go to my father and speak up. I was scared, but knew that I needed to do something to save myself. I staggered downstairs and went into my dad's office and said, "Dad, I need help. I need help now." He looked at me and knew that I was in severe distress, and took my request seriously.

Dad carried me to the car and we drove to Beth Israel Hospital in Boston, where I spoke to and was evaluated by a team of doctors and psychiatrists. When the nurse came around to take my order for dinner, I refused to eat. They brought me food anyway, but I remember looking at it and refusing. My mind was completely elsewhere.

I ended up staying at the hospital for about fourteen hours, and was actually released to go home that night. That hospital visit made me realize how out of control my problems had become, and made me realize I needed to fix them if I wanted to feel any sense of normalcy again. I needed to break up with this damned eating disorder.

I also in that moment realized how lucky and blessed I was not to have been sent for inpatient care. Because of having loved ones around me at that time, I physically was healthy enough to be at home, even though emotionally I was a wreck.

It may seem totally ludicrous that it took me so long to realize I needed help. But in this situation your mind becomes so warped that your thoughts and actions cannot help getting in the way of your healing. You do not want to let go of the eating disorder even if you are well aware of the fact that you have one. This is because the eating disorder feels like the only coping mechanism you have for dealing with what is going on deep within you and troubling you. In a completely twisted way, it brings you a sense of comfort.

Like how, no matter what, a girl will not leave a relationship with an abusive boyfriend, you stay because it is all that you know, and you feel secure having it.

What that hospital visit showed me was that although I had hit one of my lowest points, I was going to be okay. Even though there was no way I could have known this at the time, I asked for help. I surrendered to my disorder. I knew I not only needed, but wanted change, even if what that would look like was going to take a while longer for me to figure out. I knew that I was willing to change and I was pleading for help because I was sick of constantly feeling like shit. I wanted my life back.

CHAPTER NINE

Positive Role Models

*"We must learn to live together as brothers or
perish together as fools."*

—Martin Luther King, Jr.

After my visit to the hospital I began opening up and
having several conversations with different people
and adults who I look up to tremendously. I was able
to share what I had been dealing with, while gaining a sense
of empowerment from being able to speak with them about
my struggles.

For anyone entering recovery from anything, believe me I
know how hard it is to admit these things to yourself let alone
other people at first. What I have found though, is that by talking to others and opening up to safe people—non-shaming

and supportive people whom you can trust to be respectful with the information—you are choosing to live. You are setting yourself free. You are standing up to your challenges and making the decision not to let them control your life.

You have the power you need to stop the cycle of your addiction, but you have to realize this before change can happen. Finding strength during your weakest hours is one of the most challenging things in this world. But once you discover a way of doing that, the clouds will slowly start to break and the light of life will begin to emerge again.

I am very grateful to the people who were willing to listen to me, and for comforting me when I felt so alone. I am appreciative of them for giving me hope, for helping me realize I am okay, and that what has happened was also okay. For telling me I am worthy. For showing me hope for a better life. They know who they are. Without them, I would not have been able to come out of this and be who I am now. Those who listened to me and showed me their unconditional love and support are people I truly aspire to grow up to be like. I would not have been able to get through what I have without these role models in my life.

One of these people told me how important it is to have adult role models in your life who are not your parents. I have learned that having these positive role models, no matter who they are, is incredibly important for the healing process, especially for knowing that you are not alone and that you are loved unconditionally.

Although I slowly gained strength from sharing my story, I still felt very lost and unsure of where I belonged, where I should go, and where I was even going the next fall. Would I be back at NYU or somewhere else? I was by no means healed, and had a long, long way to go in my recovery.

My parents, doctors, and the therapists I was seeing at the time all were advising me that I should not go back to college. But I felt my depression and anxiety building even more at the thought of being stuck at home and essentially becoming a bum sitting on a couch all day long while all my friends and other people my age whom I knew were out fulfilling their destinies at college. I needed and wanted to move forward. I was determined for change. I felt I could not be stuck in the limbo of knowing literally nothing and having no reason to live—no purpose. I wanted to go back to school, even if that meant going back to NYU where my troubles had started.

At the time I made this decision, I realized that while what I would make of my future was up to me, I could not deal with my eating disorder on my own. I needed professional help. I needed sage advice in an ongoing manner. I needed love from those who know me best.

Once I realized that recovery was something that I am not going to go through on my own, I felt more hopeful. I decided for once to allow myself to be taken care of, to let other people be responsible for taking care of me. I knew I needed to accept help.

For anyone currently struggling with any issue in your life, I strongly encourage you to take a risk not only to ask for help, but to accept the help that is offered. Accept the fact that you NEED for once to allow other people to take care of you.

Although frightening, once you take this first step of acceptance of your needs, you are giving yourself permission to heal. Things will start to get better. As long as you do something positive to heal, no matter how small it may be, you are embarking on a road to recovery.

We all are deserving of help, yet learning that it is okay to ask for it is incredibly daunting. Do not go through life's challenges on your own. Asking for help does not mean you are a failure; it, in fact, is a demonstration of inner strength and bravery.

If you are part of a support system for people going through a challenging time, I would like to emphasize how okay it is not to know exactly what to do. None of us truly ever does. This is true even if you are just a friend who is helping another friend deal with the sadness of a breakup, for example. Nothing we say can ever be perfect. No one person alone can fix everything for someone else. Furthermore, it is not, nor is it ever, your job to fix someone else's broken situation. You do not have to know what to say.

Simply listening to someone speak about their feelings and thoughts is a gift and can be enough for someone to change the way she feels in that moment.

One of the first people I asked for help with was my lifeguarding boss. The faith he had in me gave me faith in myself. By opening up to him, I was able slowly to see my own strength and the inner power I had that others could see to which I was blind. I realized I could get through this even though, ironically, I had no idea what I was going to do.

One day, he said, "Have you ever considered studying education? I know it may not be what you ultimately end up doing, but you would, without a doubt, kill it as a teacher."

I thought about this for a while. Yes, there was a part of me that had considered teaching, but I did not know if that truly was what I wanted to do forever. How did people actually decide what they want to do in life?

Thinking about education more and more, I realized how happy and fulfilling being around children made me. I laugh now thinking about how long it took me to realize this because I have always been a teacher in a sense. I am the oldest kid in my family, and all of the jobs and activities I've engaged in have revolved around kids.

Then it hit me for real. The one thing that gave me joy during my summer of sadness was being surrounded by children when I was teaching swimming. I felt full, happy, and accomplished from seeing the progress of the kids. It made me proud when they did well.

I realized that whether or not a teacher is what I end up becoming, at least it is something that makes me truly happy right now. I also realized that helping people and helping people succeed by themselves is what I want to do.

One day I was trying to teach a little girl to blow bubbles under water. She was refusing. She cried, complained about the cold water, and was adamant about not even putting her face in the water. I held her hands, looked her in the eyes, and said, "You can do this. We are doing it together. We will be mermaids together!" Hearing these words, she smiled, laughed, and without hesitation flawlessly proceeded to submerge herself beneath the surface of the water and blow bubbles like a real mermaid.

I decided that if I went back to NYU, I would have to go back with a new major geared towards helping others, and the major I chose was childhood education.

Thanks to my boss, I was able to see my first glimmer of hope. That gave me something to look forward to: a fresh possibility that I could be really good at something new gave me a lot of joy and inspiration. Although I had never felt truly confident about doing anything, seeing the confidence others had in me as a potential teacher was enough to give me some confidence in myself.

Knowing others believe in you can truly change the way you see yourself. However, it is very important that before others believe in you, you believe in yourself and REALIZE your own strength and talents no matter how hard they may be to see at first. Being honest with others is incredibly important; however, you must be honest with yourself and be willing to seek help while embracing all of who you are.

You will be amazed by the empowerment you get when opening up to others. It truly will transform not only the way people look at you and your strength, but the way you look at yourself. You are loved, never forget that.

CHAPTER TEN

One Step
Forward, Two
Steps Back

*"Courage does not always roar. Sometimes courage is
the quiet voice at the end of the day saying,
I will try again tomorrow."*

—Mary Anne Radmacher

After my visit to the hospital, I was determined that everything would be okay. I thought I had got the eating disorder out of my system. I thought I had reached my worst, and that I would be able to wake up the next day, start over, and would be cured.

I was wrong, very wrong indeed.

The thing about eating disorders is that a rigidity of thought about life comes along with them. This element of your mindset needs to be broken. And this habit takes a long time to break. Nothing is perfect. So we really have to learn how not to be rigid or we get upset too easily. I have realized that setbacks are inevitably going to be part of recovery. It is learning how to deal with these setbacks that will separate you from someone trapped in their problems and someone who is emerging on the other side.

After my day spent in the hospital, I had many setbacks. My parents might even tell you that I was progressively getting worse at home then I was before. Each and every day after that became more and more difficult for me to get through. I felt trapped in a hurricane of darkness and misery.

Because of my pain, gradually I came to accept that my problems would not go away without treatment. Like any illness, for the most part you cannot just wake up after going to the doctor and be cured. Cancer does not just go away. A broken leg does not magically mend just because you put a cast on it. If I wanted to change, I needed to work for it.

The scariest part of starting the recovery process is letting go of what you know, and also realizing that for just a little while you HAVE TO be *incredibly* selfish. You have to take time out from whatever it is you are doing to care for yourself and find love within yourself. You need to allow your heart and your spirit to heal. To do this fully, you must be selfish.

For me, this approach seemed impossible and straight up felt wrong. I had never put myself or my health first before others, other things, or other responsibilities. I was terribly uncomfortable with the idea of stopping my activities while I worked on my recovery. I did not want to stop living the life

I thought I had at the time. I did not believe any form of treatment or help could actually ever fix me. Basically, I believed I was a lost cause.

I was embarrassed by needing to miss work to deal with what I was going through. I did not want anyone to think I was neglecting my responsibilities. I also did not know how I would be able to explain to coworkers and the parents at the pool why I suddenly wasn't around or acting like the Lucy they all knew and loved. However, it was impressed upon me by my doctors and parents that if I did not take the time to accept my circumstances in front of me and get treatment I would not be able to do anything else. If I did not address the eating disorder, there would never be room in my life for things that matter and make me truly happy. An eating disorder consumes and destroys your real life while filling it with a fake world that is enveloped in misery.

Although I definitely did not believe her at first, my mom was right when she told me, "Lucy, you are giving yourself the greatest gift. If you willingly accept this help, you will emerge better then you ever have been before."

I finally consented to treatment and began seeing a therapist on a weekly basis and a registered dietician specializing in nutritional therapy for people coming out of eating disorders on a weekly basis, as well as a doctor and medical team who continually tracked my weight and overall progress. Accepting their professional help and slowly letting go of my eating disorder was the hardest thing I have ever done in my life. But I did it because I wanted to be normal and healthy. I wanted to know what it felt like to be happy. I wanted to live a genuine life.

The truth of the matter is that you will truly never be able to live the life you want if you have an active eating disorder.

If this part remains active inside of you there simply won't be enough room for the real you to exist. The eating disorder becomes your life.

So you must ask yourself if life with anorexia, bulimia, or an eating disorder is the life you truly want to live: being alone all the time, having your thoughts consumed with nothing but food, constantly tearing yourself and your body image down. Missing out on family activities, on friendships, and on forming irreplaceable relationships with others. Not having a reason to live. Not allowing yourself to live, grow, develop, and experience life.

Not wanting to face and contribute to the beautiful world we all live in? This is not living.

I knew I could no longer live with an eating disorder as my reality. I wanted more.

As much as I wanted to change, actually implementing that change takes a really long time. It does happen though. If you're in recovery, you must be patient with the process. Although I recognized my need and desire for this change, my setbacks continued. These setbacks were essential parts of the recovery.

Through the progression of the summer and the acceptance of help, my setbacks continued to occur and my depression actually worsened as the prospect of school came nearer and nearer. I wanted to go back to college, but was becoming furiously angry and frustrated because everyone helping me kept advising me not to go back to school. I wanted to live. I wanted to move forward, but I felt that I was being held back. I was certain I knew what truly was best for me no matter what the experts were telling me.

Now, if you are someone in the midst of an eating disorder, please understand that I am by no means encouraging you to stay in school against the advice of your counselors. In fact, for many people of college age, taking a break from school is essential for them to recover. Like my mom said, you will be giving yourself the greatest gift you could ever receive by taking time to heal. For me, however, I needed to move forward and I did not feel I could do that if I was "trapped" in my past at home. I decided what was best for me and the needs of my healing process.

With that being said, however, I moved forward under the agreement that I would have help and with a team set up for me in New York City. Since returning to school I have gone to therapy sessions three times a week. I am seeing both a psychologist and a registered dietitian, and I travel back to Boston every so often to check in with the medical doctor there as well.

While at times it is still incredibly difficult for me to be in recovery, and I get mad for not feeling like a "normal" college student, I know that at this point in my life this level of professional care is what I need to be doing. I am considering this new self-care part of my job as a student. I am learning how important it is and should be. And I am realizing that I am not selfish or abnormal for taking time to care for myself.

I am by no means undermining the advice the experts back home gave me. I am thankful for these people each and every day. I thank God for putting them in my life in my state of crisis. But I knew I needed to leave home even if I was getting worse in that present moment.

Recently I was thinking back to my darkest day at the end of the summer. It was not the hospital visit or the times I was so malnourished I could not walk or get out of bed because of a lack of energy. My darkest day occurred on August 22, right before I was to go back to school. My lifeguarding job was over and I no longer was teaching swimming. Many of my friends had already gone back to college. That's when I felt completely alone and most uncertain about what was to come.

That day, I wrote in my journal:

I just binged so much that I cannot move. Pain is filling
my body. I know though that I cannot make myself
throw up. I need to get better. I can feel my legs,
fingers, and stomach growing more and more bloated.
I cannot stop eating. I feel like I am going to die, and I
pray to die. Take me right now, I will be better off.
I currently cannot get off the floor of my bedroom in
darkness. I am alone. No one hears my crying, no one
sees my tears. My hair is matted. My teeth are not
brushed. I cannot bring myself even to take a shower or
get myself to change my clothes. I have been wearing
the same dress for the past three days.

That day I reached my lowest point. I emotionally was in such pain that I could not move. I was packed to go to school the next day. But how would that ever be possible? I did not know, I only knew I wanted to be anywhere else but there. Before I went to sleep that night, wearing that same dress with tear stains smeared and stuck to my cheeks, I prayed to die in my dreams.

CHAPTER ELEVEN

A New Day

*"There is no magic cure, no making it all go away
forever. There are only small steps upward;
an easier day, an unexpected laugh, a mirror that
doesn't matter anymore."*

—Laurie Anderson

I woke up on the morning of August 23rd and immediately had a panic attack. Then I ate uncontrollably at breakfast. I was a wreck. In the back of my mind, however, I knew that the potential of school coming meant I could make a new start.

I do not know how, considering how freaked out I was, but I was able to find the strength to take a shower and clean myself up. I put on a fresh set of clothes, got in the car with my mom, and then we embarked on our journey to move me into a new dorm room in New York City.

My mood was improving, and although the thought of going to New York was giving me extreme anxiety I was hoping that it would at least be a possible release from feeling like I have no motivation to do anything.

My mom and I set up my dorm room, and then went to grab a quick dinner at a cute restaurant in Greenwich Village. Mom was spending the first night in a hotel nearby in case something happened. My classes actually were not set to start for another week, but I was supposed to be an orientation leader for the freshman welcome week at NYU.

The next morning, I woke up, got dressed for Welcome Week, and what do you guess happened? My good old friend anxiety came knocking at my door and brought along with it a massive panic attack as a house warming gift. I broke down and was uncontrollably sobbing. I couldn't do it. I could not be a Welcome Week leader. I could not be at school. I was not strong enough. My new day suddenly turned to night, because the unending darkness had returned.

My mother picked me up, put my stuff in the car, and we returned to my hometown. This was it. "I am such a loser," I kept saying over and over again to her the whole way home.

CHAPTER TWELVE

Take Two?

*"Never say goodbye because goodbye means going
away and going away means forgetting."*

—J.M Barrie

After my failure to launch, I went home and spent time with my therapists. I also spent a lot of time reflecting by myself. On August 27, I was able to celebrate my sister's and my dad's birthdays, and think more about what I wanted and was going to do in the future.

I continued to have setbacks and days where I could not get up off of the couch. One thing that saved me during one of these moments of crisis was how one night a family friend, Maura, came over and took me to Ikea. We picked out pillows and then sewed pillow cases out of my favorite pale pink fabric. I am forever grateful for Maura and that night. I could not have stood up without her by my side. I love her.

Why did this matter so much? The pillows inspired me. I wanted to see those pillows in the living room of my dorm in

New York City. Part of me still could not let go of going to school. I needed to try it to see. If I failed again, I would then know for certain.

Looking back at where I was, I literally have no idea how I was able to gain the strength to go back and try again, or how my parents found the faith in me to allow me to go back. For one thing, going back meant returning to the place that had caused my life to begin spiraling out of control. And for another thing, one could argue that clinically I was so unstable that I was physically, mentally, and emotionally incapable of going to school.

Something in my gut continually was telling me to go back nonetheless. I do not know why. Some may argue I was absolutely nuts in listening to that voice. Even I was in constant conflict within myself about the fact that I was choosing to return after I had tried and could not even handle Welcome Week—a week with no classes. I wanted to push forward though. I felt I needed to keep trying. I know that at times I am way too hard on myself, but this was something I knew I needed, no matter how irrational it seemed to try.

I got in the car for the second time a week later and embarked on my second journey to NYU—this time with my new homemade pillows. Yes, I was very anxious, but I felt slightly better.

That second car ride with Mom was kind of funny. We laughed, we cried, we sang, we prayed. As we got closer and the New York City skyline came in view, I remember yelling, "WHAT THE HECK AM I DOING? AM I ABSOLUTELY OUT OF MY MIND COMING BACK HERE?!"

I don't know how, but I was able to find so much humor in my situation that day. I could not stop laughing, to the point that tears were streaming down my face. I said out loud,

"Yup, I am a freaking anorexic who has just shoveled four pancakes and a large dairy twist ice cream down my throat in order to cope with my stress."

I said, "Yup, I have been severely depressed and suicidal the past few months."

I also said, "Yup, I am completely insane because I am returning to the place that ignited the fire of my past crazy year and I believe this is the best choice I could ever possibly make right now."

I truly was laughing my ass off. I think all the laughing was my reaction to the utter terror that was actually inside my heart. I literally did not know how to cope so I made jokes about my situation. The entire ride I felt like I was in a dream.

I did not want my mom to get out of the car when she dropped me off. Saying goodbye to anyone is one of my weaknesses, as I despise change. I just cannot do it easily. It kills me inside. Even when it's a friend, cousin, or grandmother I know I'll see again. I hate knowing that when you say goodbye you are not going to see that person the next day. Tears even are filling my eyes as I write this sentence while thinking of the feelings I get every time I say goodbye to someone I love.

I try to avoid goodbyes as much as I can, as they are just too hard for me.

So that was it. My mom pulled up to the corner of Fourteenth Street and Third Avenue. I gave her a hug in the car, and she cried while saying to me, "Letting go this time around is oddly a thousand times harder for me then it was last year."

In retrospect I don't know how she ever did it.

I know I am not a mother yet, but the thought of pulling up to the concrete jungle of Manhattan and letting out your child who is in so much pain so she can go back into the midst of the place that caused so much of her pain must have felt like straight-up inflicted child abuse.

But I told her, "I'll see you soon," and got out of the car, trying with every ounce of strength in my body not to fall apart in front of her. I had to do this. I had to be strong for both of us, and in order to do so, I could not say goodbye.

CHAPTER THIRTEEN

Rebirth

*"The flower that blooms in adversity, is the most rare
and beautiful flower of all"*

—Mulan

On August 31st, I arrived for my second chance at sophomore year. The first thing I did when I got to my dorm room was go for a swim. I am one lucky little duck getting to live in the middle of Manhattan with a gorgeous swimming pool and athletic facility in my building. It truly is something you would imagine only possibly in movies.

That particular swim for me symbolized my rebirth. A fresh start. Washing away, in a sense, my pain from the past. I knew this did not mean that there would not be other setbacks and pain in the future, but for the time being this was the biggest step I had taken. You see, I had not exercised in close to a month because of how horrible my depression had become. Thus I was so proud of my accomplishment. And my body felt a little better.

Being physically healthy is a reflection of how you are doing on the inside emotionally. Although my health was not perfect at that time, I felt so much better and closer to being myself then I had in a long while. This is when I knew staying in New York for the time being was what I had to do, even if it meant that more bumps and challenges were to come.

When I went up to my room I was greeted by three of the most loving, comforting, and welcoming roommates I could have ever imagined possible. These were girls I had met the previous year and was so lucky to have grown closer with. They embraced me fully. For the first time since being at home with my family in Massachusetts, I felt like I had a place where I belonged and could feel safe. I was finding what I now know is what college should feel like for people, a home away from home. A place where you are loved. A place where you can be who you are and be unconditionally accepted by those around you.

My heart and everything around me kept telling me I was going to make it, regardless of how hard this transition would be. I knew I could do it and get through it with grace. I knew I was in a healthy, positive, new, and nurturing environment in my room. I knew childhood education would be a passionate subject of learning that I would thrive at studying.

Although I was in a new environment and had the possibility of a fresh start, it did not occur for me instantly. I continued to have setbacks. And let's be honest, we all will from time to time, no matter where we are or what we are doing in our lives! Challenges inevitably arise.

There are no quick fixes for matters that run as deep as eating disorders do. After a few days at school my depression sort of set in again, and the initial excitement and energy I had about starting over seemed to diminish.

This phenomenon is very common for anyone getting over something, therefore it is important to try to remember to stay passionate, and to have faith that the passion will return. Good days inevitably will be followed by bad days, but we can know that through hard work and perseverance, slowly but surely, the good days start to outnumber the bad ones.

A technique I learned from therapy was that if you cannot feel good, you can at least try to remember and visualize your happiest day. The day that you were passionate, the day you felt immersed and surrounded by love. Remember the feelings you felt on that specific day and things do get better. When you hit rock bottom, you cannot go anywhere but up.

If you do not mind, I would like to share a journal entry that represented the constant up and down emotions I was feeling being back in New York.

Yesterday and today have been incredibly difficult. I also just do not have the words even to know how to express this to my family. It is so hard to convey all that I am feeling to others in a way that they will understand. I think Mom is going away with Rory, the last thing I want to do is put any burden or concern on her. We all have that on our own as it is. I also really don't want to upset or worry Dad in any way. He just caught his first tuna fish while fishing with his best friend from college and I really do not want to suck the joy away from that moment for him.

It makes me sad I haven't heard from them during the past few days. Mia texts me every day though, and although I have trouble articulating where I am at, it

*makes me feel very loved and comforted by her. I can't
thank Big Brenda and little Brenda enough for taking
me in and welcoming me open heartedly into their
homes whenever I need.*

*My anxiety has been beyond awful. Yesterday
especially. But I am still doing everything in my power
to stay strong. I woke up this morning not knowing if I
could do this. Questioning everything. Barely able to
get dressed. I forced myself on a run, then cleaned up,
and then walked to Kimmel Hall on campus, and now I
am currently writing this. I feel a little stronger after
expressing all of these feelings on paper. I am going to
try to take on this world. I guess we will have to wait
and see for what happens.*

If you notice the difference between this and the other
journal entry I shared with earlier in the book (see page 68)
you can see the progression I was slowly making. Even
though I was still feeling immense pain, I had more hope and
motivation then before.

You have the strength to find this as well if you're
struggling with food issues. Believe me, if I could make
progress, so can you. It may seems impossible now, but please
just try. I promise with all of my heart that putting in any
amount of effort of to live your life despite feeling anxious, no
matter how small a step you take may be, will be rewarding.

CHAPTER FOURTEEN

Miracles Are Real

"Miracles are a retelling in small letters of the very same story which is written across the whole world in letters too large for some of us to see."

—C.S. Lewis

One of the most powerful things I have learned during my recovery is that we can experience magic in our darkest moments. I'm being deadly serious. You may not believe me, and I do not expect you to—for crying out loud I am only a college kid. But I can say with complete certainty that through these times of darkness I was able to see glimpses of power, light, and magic that do not present themselves regularly in most of our everyday lives.

I guess I could always say that I have had a faith. I have always believed in a higher power, and have thought that there must be something greater than us here on earth. However, I have never been what you would say to be very religious.

I was raised Catholic and got baptized and confirmed in a Catholic church, but to be honest, I really do not know all that much about religion. And perhaps it is something I will explore more down the road. I really do not feel I have the knowledge or credibility to talk about religion because I have struggled to fully understand it myself. What I have realized though, is that this is totally okay. God loves me unconditionally regardless of how much I know about God. I do not even necessarily mean to use the word *God* here because I feel like it has a connotation everyone will just tie religion. I want to emphasize that I am not talking about religion here. I am talking about my faith in what lies beyond what we see in front of us.

I am taking time to write about this because I believe faith and hope saved my life.

I have noticed that people who experience a strong renewal of their faith come to this realization after times when life puts them through its trials. I do not think any of us can pinpoint why that exactly is. However, I speculate that it is because we have no other way of understanding the tragedies that occur. Our lack of understanding is due to the deep pain these trials inflict. We cannot understand why bad things happen.

Why do we live in a world of war? Why are there terrorist attacks periodically occurring on our soil? Why is there cancer? Why is the fight for equality not even close to being over in this day and age? Why are people racist? Why are people discriminated against for loving who they love? Why are people starving and living on the streets? Why do we hate? Why is there violence? Why are our loved ones entangled with inner demons of drugs, alcohol, and abusive relationships? Why do those we love die? Why are innocent children abandoned by their own mothers and fathers? Why do people endure unfixable injuries that incapacitate them forever? Why does it seem we constantly have to say goodbye to what we love? Why? Why? Why?

All of these questions challenge our humanity.

I cannot answer, nor can anyone know, why terrible challenges continue to arise. I know that it is things like these that make many people lose their faith.

Speaking for myself, the challenges I have seen and faced have shown me that hardships create opportunities to show love. They give us something more to find, a way to show our strength and somehow help others in their own struggles. These challenges create the opportunity for us to unite and help each other through unconditional love. I know many people believe that not everything happens for a reason, but I think that if you allow yourself to think that each event does have reason you will slowly begin to see beyond yourself and have an open perspective. Having faith has taught me this.

Within my battle, I felt alone. I felt I had no one to turn to. I felt I could not rely on anyone to fully understand what I was going through. As a result, I turned to the only thing I could imagine that would understand what I was going through. I turned to prayer.

As I have said before, I am not even entirely sure what I was praying to. I called it God, but for you this force might be called something different. I prayed every minute of every day, and I knew I was being heard. I prayed to God, I prayed to angels, and I prayed to my relatives who have passed away.

I asked for signs, and I asked to know I was not alone in my struggle. I knew that they heard me because I saw signs I had never seen before.

I knew that the signs I saw, things I heard, and dreams I had were God speaking and reaching out directly to me. God was comforting me. When I tell people about the signs, not many understand or take what I say literally. However, I know what I know. I know what I have seen. Because of this I stand stronger each day, knowing that I am never alone. I want to thank all of my angels for showing me your love when I asked, and for never abandoning me, especially during a time when I felt abandoned by everyone here on Earth.

As I have grown stronger, I have learned that God has been with me all along. Our angels are with all of us each and every day, and are constantly giving us signs. However, for many of us it just takes being in a state of utmost vulnerability to be able to come to terms and acknowledge these signs. So just know that they are there. And not only are they there, they are real and true-life miracles.

I also think it is very easy to play off signs from God as mere coincidences that you can laugh off and just think, *Oh, that's funny.* Know they are real. I promise. They are God's ways of showing that you are loved. I swear.

I want to give you a few examples so you know what I mean when I say a *sign* or a *miracle*, and so you can look and start to be aware of these little things in your own daily life. You don't have to be in pain to see God's love.

I am not going to share all the signs I saw because I want to keep some of what has come to me private. However, I am going to share with you one of my journal entries written on a day I saw angels and heard God speaking to me.

August 14

*Today I had a nutrition appointment, and then later a
therapy session. In nutrition, we were talking about the
importance of carbohydrates in your diet. Why they are
essential, why we need them to survive, and why so
often we get distorted thoughts about "carbs" because
of how the media and so many people play them off to
be. I went home after that and knew it was lunch time. I
was kind of anxious and wanted to resort to my "safe
choice," however I saw in the fridge there was left-over
angel hair pasta with a little bit of oil on it, and fresh
grilled shrimp. The thought of eating pasta makes me so
scared of getting fat, but I know my therapist would
remind me that this was my eating disorder speaking
and not really me.*

*My body needed carbohydrates and I needed to
listen to it in order to realign my mind with my physical
needs. Okay, I took the risk and ate the damned pasta. I
cannot remember the last time I ate pasta. I have never
really been a pasta girl. Way more of a bread and pizza
girl, but this pasta tasted pretty good and I was able to
see the nutritional value in it without total distortion.
Okay, so then I went to my therapy appointment. I was
really scared, anxious about what I had just ate, and
felt sad and overwhelmed with my depression.*

*While waiting in the waiting room, I opened up a
magazine and sitting in front of me was a page that
read: "Lucy's magic ANGEL hair pasta recipe." Pictured next to the title was a little girl with long, curly
hair eating the pasta. She kind of looked like me with
my long curly blond hair. I paused, smiled, and felt the*

energy of unconditional love around me. I knew this
was a sign from an angel. I could feel the angel with
me.

I hadn't eaten angel pasta in years, and that
afternoon I happened to, and then open up to that
random page in that random magazine? This could not
have been a coincidence!

Thank you, God, for showing me I am not alone.

That is one example where I was able to see God's love. Another time happened at college. My mom forwarded a letter to me that had been sent to our house in Massachusetts. It was addressed to "The Real Lucy Quigley." Inside was some sort of advertisement, however the letter was addressed specifically to "Princess Lucy" and contained a beyond uplifting message that emphasized strength, love, belief in possibilities, and the importance of inner beauty. There was no source of where this letter came from.

This letter was delivered to me during midterms when I was having a really hard time emotionally. I knew it was from an angel and that God was speaking directly to me.

Listen for signs as well, as they may not always be obvious. Look for messages and listen to words that resonate with YOU within lyrics of songs. Once you open yourself up to this, your possibilities are endless, and I promise you will hear more messages and realize how loved you are.

One of my other big signs is feathers. I have heard that feathers specifically are from angels or your loved ones that have passed away. However, I find in times of stress I will pray for a feather as a sign and my angels have never failed to deliver. God's honest truth.

Lastly I want to talk about my good friend Susie who passed away in November 2016. Susie was the most beautiful mother of five of the greatest children I ever had the privilege of knowing. She was a hilarious, lively, and talented woman who was NEVER afraid to speak her mind. She always tried to toughen me up in a sense.

The day Susie passed away, I was walking along Fifth Avenue and passing Saint Patrick's Cathedral. Unfortunately, with the world we live in today, as a young girl alone in Manhattan I do have to take my personal safety into consideration, especially when walking alone at night. This night, three big men, who were all twice my size, came up to me and started hassling me and yelling derogatory comments to me about my body. They also made fun of the pink backpack I had on.

I am not going to lie, the visual was pretty comical. I was wearing a pink dress with a pink jacket, and a pink bow in my hair.

Usually in these types of situations I just ignore the guys, I run away, or I quickly cross the street. Something felt different though. I don't know what came over me, but I felt strong inside. I stopped, turned around, stood as tall as I could with my pink backpack and screamed on the top of my lungs on the street in front of probably about fifty other people, "EXCUSE ME. FUCK OFF AND LEAVE ME ALONE."

I was so proud of myself! I knew, however, that it was Susie coming through me and teaching me to stand up for myself, even though she wasn't physically there. I felt her with me. She was protecting me and she was so proud of me for telling those dummies to take a hike. Susie always taught me and everyone that it was okay to use your voice and throw in a few eff bombs now and again when needed. I swear I had never ever had the courage or strength of doing anything like that until then. THANKS, MAMA SUS, I KNOW IT WAS REALLY ALL YOU.

Now, maybe the way God and your angels show you love will be different then the way that they show me. I don't know and I can't predict. I am certain it is different for all of us, and that we all connect to God's force in very different ways because of the differences within all of us. However, know that faith is a very real thing. Angels listen, they are there, and they want to show you their unconditional love as long as you are willing to listen.

Also, remember the ones we love who aren't here can hear you too, and they are always listening and looking out for you. Grandpa, Kevin, Gerry, Gigi, Susie, and all the rest of you up there in heaven that I have not yet had the grace to meet here on earth, I know you see me. Thank you for the love you have shown me and my family. I can't wait to see you all again sometime. I now know for certain that we never really have to say goodbye.

CHAPTER FIFTEEN

Ten Tips and Tricks for Triumphant Tenacity

"You yourself, as much as anybody in the entire universe, deserve your love and affection."

—Buddha

Has someone ever told you: "You cannot find love until you love yourself first"? Blah blah blah. I know I have been told that at least a thousand times during my recovery. But what the heck does that even mean? Slowly, I have grudgingly accepted the utter truth of this statement and the fundamental necessity of realizing it.

I hate to break it to you, but it is true. You have to love yourself if you want to find love or happiness in different areas of your life. If you do not care for yourself and for your body, and appreciate all of your successes for how big or small they may be, you won't have a reason to fully live and embrace the gifts within your beautiful life.

How do we go about loving ourselves? It is an individual process. What "loving yourself" means for me may end up being totally different than what it means for you. I am still figuring it out, and probably will continue to figure it out for the rest of my life. People I trust who are older than me tell me that we are always discovering new parts of ourselves and developing new interests our whole lives. It may take many small steps to fully love ourselves, so we need to be tenacious.

Speaking for myself, the more I try to love myself, the better I feel, and so I want to share some of the tips and tricks I have used that have brought me to the realization of the truth of this statement, which have helped me emerge from the dark.

1. **Self-care:** Self-care is probably the most important tip. For anyone getting over an eating disorder, specifically, caring for your mind and your body is essential and also can be a great distraction for taking your mind off of food. This includes taking the time to go to therapy or do whatever you need to do to get better. Some specific

smaller things I continually do when I feel stressed and vulnerable are:

- Getting my nails done or painting them myself.
- Watching a YouTube tutorial on a cool hairstyle and experimenting with doing it on myself.
- Taking a shower.
- Putting on a new outfit that makes me feel amazing and confident. This in particular, I find, can help break an old cycle. It makes me feel like I have made a new start within that very moment.

2. **Exercise:** Exercise is truly an amazing form of therapy. It clears your body of stress and tension because of the endorphins that it releases. There is nothing I love more than doing a cardio workout. However, since I have been suffering from an eating disorder, I am aware of how cautious I have to be with cardio, because of the high amount of calories that are burned. Try these:

- **Running.** For those of you who are not enveloped in the fragile state of an eating disorder, I would definitely recommend running. I also love swimming. Swimming is easier on the muscles. It works your entire body and is just as good of a cardio workout as running, but lower in impact.
- **Yoga!** Yoga, and especially the aspect of mindfulness that it develops, is transformative when applied to daily life. Mindfulness just means being consciously aware of yourself and your environment in a present moment. Being mindful and aware of your body and your surroundings is so important for all of us.

For those who struggle with eating disorders, even more so. Mindfulness is truly like medicine! The key is being able to reconnect your mind with what your body is telling you it needs. Hunger, thirst, movement. Of course, this lesson is applicable to everyone, not just those of us with eating disorders. Put down your cellphone and be aware of what and who is in front of you.

Being mindful promotes growth in all aspects of your life. It can improve your interpersonal relationships, your ability to listen, follow, and engage in conversations, even your success in school. Your grades can be improved with mindfulness. I highly recommend doing yoga and having a daily mindfulness practice such as meditation.

- **Meditation:** A self-care activity that I did and try to do often throughout my recovery. Meditation is one of the easiest ways to practice mindfulness. During moments of severe anxiety doing meditation can ease some of the suffering. The simplest way is to sit and set a timer for five minutes, close your eyes, relax your body, and focus on your breath. There also are wonderful free resources for guided meditation practices. I use the free app Insight often, you also can go on to YouTube and type in guided meditation to help.
- **Dance:** I am by no means a good dancer. Hahaha. In fact, I'm kind of awkward. But for me, dancing to blasting music while acting like a complete idiot is incredibly therapeutic! Twerking against the wall, doing handstands and cartwheels, or doing

flips on my trampoline at home can give me a massive outlet.

The best time I remember is when my sister Mia joined me and we screamed at the top of our lungs to Justin Bieber's song "YOU SHOULD GO AND <u>LOVE YOURSELF.</u>" (See what I did there?) and danced like no one in the world could watch us.

- **Walking.** Taking a walk really clears the mind. Walk to some place that feels like a safe haven for YOU, one that means something, and just go there. The walking helps you to at least move, and going to a place you appreciate will make you feel safe. Maybe it's at the beach, in the woods, at a pond, or visiting a good friend's home. Forcing yourself to GET OUT though is the huge tip. Creating a change of scenery brings you back to reality and reorganizes the disordered thoughts within your head.

3. **Gratitude**: Most recently, this tool has been the absolute most effective one I have used in order to feel better. I use it to snap myself out of a dark place. It has even helped me handle the overpowering urges of my eating disorder. What I do, when I start feeling unstable, is pause, reflect for the moment about where I am, and then find something to be grateful for—even if it's just a beautiful ceiling in the room. I say to myself, "Wow, the color of that paint is gorgeous," "I am so thankful to have this roof over my head," or "I am grateful to have this beautiful moment of solitude and peace." Gratitude really helps me feel better.

Or if I'm at a meal with foods that seem scary, I pause, breathe, and think, *I am so thankful for being with my family, whom I don't get to see every day, and for feeling love and a glimmer of happiness.* Sometimes I also think back to my darkest moment and remind myself that I am not there anymore, and that I have the power to prevent myself from ever going back to that place again.

Remembering where we are and that somewhere there is always someone who has it worse than us is another mental trick that can help us appreciate where we are in the moment a little more.

Having gratitude for the present state brings us back to real life and helps decrease the level of anxiety within us that may become fuel for a binge, purge, or any other method of self-harming behavior we might feel an urge to engage in.

4. **Singing:** I do not know the exact reasoning behind this trick, but I know that for me something about singing makes me really happy. Now, granted, I am not always be in the mood to sing, and sometimes I am way too sad to sing or even to speak. But when I do open my mouth when I am feeling well enough, something about singing and music resonates deep within my soul and this helps me feel better and more capable.

5. **Song writing:** Song writing also became an outlet for me when I started recovery. I really love writing lyrics about whatever I am feeling, and putting tunes to the words. I love going on GarageBand and making mashups of my favorite songs. You definitely don't need to be musical or know how to play instruments to do this! All you really need is access to a computer. Try

expressing yourself through sound and creation of music. You could be surprised by how much you will learn about what you are feeling in the moment.

I may have mentioned earlier how I used to play the violin. For me, playing the violin was too hard during this vulnerable time because it brought forth too many emotions for me. Nonetheless, I felt I needed to fill the gap of music in my life. So I messed around on the piano and picked out the notes of songs that I heard in my head. I also picked up the ukulele and learned to sing along with that, playing basic chords. My point is, you know what you need. Follow yourself and what your inner voice tells you. And do not be discouraged when you cannot do it all. I am sure there will come a day when I will play the violin again.

6. **Listening to a complete album from start to finish**. This was a very therapeutic technique for me. I would pick an album and allow myself to get completely enveloped in the story the artist was telling. I would relate myself to them, and give myself permission to feel all that they were feeling, and to listen, cry, and learn that things would be okay.

I know music is not everyone's thing. Maybe you can have a similar experience by getting totally enveloped in a movie, or book, or even a TV show. I am not encouraging that you shut yourself in and watch thirty-six straight hours of Netflix, but give yourself permission while to get wrapped up in something for a little that you enjoy. You will feel better for the time being if you do.

7. **Writing**: The last creative outlet I am going to talk about is writing. When some people think of writing,

there is an academic connotation associated with it. But I think it is fun. If you think of it as a burden, for a second just pretend this isn't so and erase all of that for your mind. Take out a pencil or a pen and a piece of paper and just write anything that's in your head. Writing in a journal released me and contributed hugely to my healing process. When I wrote, it set me free of anything I felt guilty of or any painful feelings or memories I was holding on to. I really encourage you to do the same so you can find out for yourself what I mean. Writing may enable you to release your worst feelings in the safest way possible.

8. **Working hard**: Even if you feel miserable in working hard, this tip pays off in the future. It's like a gift you give your future self. Although during my freshman year of college I was miserable and unsatisfied with my classes and schoolwork, I worked my butt off and got the best grades I could. If I had not done this, I would not have been allowed to switch disciplines to childhood education. My grade point average and standing with the university permitted me to be an exception and to complete this change at the last minute. Please just know that whatever you are doing, it is important to do it wholeheartedly because it will likely pay off in ways that you wouldn't think possible until they happen.

9. **Reaching Out to Others.** I want to discuss the importance of reaching out in times of need. THIS IS SO DIFFICULT. Believe me, I know. I have been there. In that moment when you are lying in the fetal position on the floor of your bedroom, crouched over a toilet in the bathroom about to purge, stuck with a

bottle of vodka in your hands, or frozen with a razor about to cut yourself, remember that you are never, ever alone. Calling or texting someone, or even Snapchatting with someone, will make you feel better. You cannot, nor should you ever have to feel what you are feeling all on your own. And you don't have to! In the Resources section of this book, I have provided some ideas about how you can start getting help to realize that you ARE loved Even if it doesn't seem like it yet. loving yourself by knowing to reach out will slowly, but surely help you to heal.

I know that in difficult moments choosing to be alone can seem way easier. But that is not living. Life is not easy. Making the harder choice, while painful for internally in this moment, is essential if you want to be truly better and feel better in the long term. We were not placed on earth to be alone. With counseling, I have realized the importance of connection and maintaining connections throughout my healing process. Choose to live, choose to be with others, choose love.

10. **Setting a Timer.** When you are about to hurt yourself in whatever way—whether that is cutting, binge eating, vomiting, drinking, smoking, whatever—**set a timer.** Delay the self-harm as LONG as possible. Start with five minutes. During those five minutes, do a self-care activity. It could be any of the ones I mentioned, or any of your own, anything that you can think of. Try to breathe, focus on your breath, and bring yourself back into the present moment.

Even if after the five minutes the original feelings return, you can still say, "You know what? I was able to stop for five minutes. That in itself is a victory." Never diminish your small victories. Celebrate them. Each one builds your inner strength, and will make you stronger for the next time.

I know my hobbies and self-care techniques are probably different from yours, but I hope that explaining them and telling you the feelings I get from each one will help you see the purpose and importance of having and USING them in times of need!

THINGS THAT MAKE ME HAPPY

Below is a list of some things to do, experience, or think about that make me happy. Perhaps some of these can help you as well! Or let them inspire you to come up with your own list of items to turn to whenever you're feeling sad or stressed.

Thinking pink
Fuzzy blankets
Mermaids
SWIMMING
Summertime
Flowers
Online fantasy shopping
Creating outfits
Going to pet shops
Bradley Cooper
Comfy clothes
Lululemon
WRITING

Uncontrollable laugh attacks
Jennifer Lawrence
Helping people
Drawing
Family
Music
Reese's[R] *peanut butter cups*
Peanut butter
Trader Joe's
Rite Aid
Snow
Christmas

Puppies
Angels
Curly hair
Rainy days
Summer thunder storms
Pumpkin spice lattes
Hot cups of coffee and tea
Homemade pizza
Christmas movies
The Parent Trap
The Last Song
Things that are old
   fashioned
Zac Efron
Ian Somerhalder
Broadway musicals
Ed Sheeran
Michelle Obama
Emma Watson
Giving gifts
Writing letters and cards
Adele
Alicia Keys
Singing songs
Carpool karaoke
Big hugs
Seeing people I haven't
   seen in a long time

Making scenes in public
Walgreens
Target
Funny voices and jokes at
   unexpected moments
Complimenting others
Aquamarine
Twerking
Love
Cozy nights by a fire
Kindness

CHAPTER SIXTEEN

Where I Am

"To live will be an awfully big adventure."

—J.M. Barrie

Thank you for reading my story and paying attention to what I have to say. My greatest hope is that my words resonate with you and your feelings.

While what I wrote earlier about NYU may have seemed like I hated the school, I want to now thank you, NYU, for not just giving me education, but for giving me a gift that has turned me into the stronger woman I am today. Because of you I have learned more about myself than ever before. I have been able to see the world at my fingertips and gain a whole new sense of empathy and understanding of life that I don't think many nineteen-year-olds are lucky enough to have.

One of the hardest aspects of the struggle with an eating disorder, in my opinion, is the loneliness of recovery. Yes, I have family and other people that love and care for me, and do their best to help me. But at the end of the day, the struggle is a personal one. It's me and my own weight (no pun intended) that I have to carry. I am the one who has to change and get better. If this is an issue you are also facing, you can find companionship, but it is also you who must do the work to get better. No matter how much caring people relate to what I am feeling or you are feeling, it is and always will be impossible for them to do the work for me or for you, because they are not you or me.

Whatever problem you face, yes it sucks. Yes, it's awful to feel alone. But try to accept others' love as it comes, even when it's not in the form that you want or would prefer. Know that while only you can ultimately fix your problem, shutting others out is only going to make things worse. Embrace the love people give you in every form it comes, even if it upsets you that they don't seem to understand what you want and need in the right way. Love is love, and life without love is not as beautiful.

On the outside, I may appear to be a smiling girl, a successful student, a leader, a sister, a teacher, a friend, a swimmer, and a musician, someone friendly and nice who shows love for everything and everyone. Yet inside and behind closed doors, I have been living in a world of suffering and darkness for several years. Often the outside and the inside do not match. And since I've been working on my issues, I am seeing more light more often. My story is changing. I have hope.

Look, I'm not saying that my personal story is the biggest tragedy that the human race has seen, by any means. I am very cognizant that compared most people around the world I am beyond privileged to receive my education and have a loving family and fresh food and water to eat and drink each and every day. So many of these basics are unjustly robbed from people or unavailable to people and I am aware of how truly blessed I am and always have been in my life.

Everyone deserves to have her basic human needs met, including her need for love and purpose. My story and my pain are real to me, and I am not going to discount or reject them. Even so, they are not my whole story.

What I hope to convey from sharing where I am today with you is that no matter what your story is or where you believe it is headed, the simple fact is that we all have a story. We all have feelings and needs. And this is why my view and approach to life is one of care, sensitivity, and demonstrating love to all. As cheesy as saying this may sound, something my Dad told me ever since I can remember is my guiding principle: "I find nothing more truthful then the importance of treating everyone in the way you wish to be treated." I guess you could call this the golden rule.

While I may not be exactly one thing or belong in only one category, I am realizing that the versatility I have within me is part of what makes me who I am, and it is what makes me special. No, I am not Yoyo Ma when I play an instrument. No, I will never be Michael Phelps in a swimming pool. But I am me. I have been learning that there is nothing possibly more worthy than being me and loving myself as I am, as opposed to striving toward a fake reality in which I am failing at being something else.

Although my story I'm sure is different from yours in some details, my wish is that in some way or another you can relate to what I have been through and that it helps you learn to accept yourself. I hope to at least be a bridge in some form for you to understand that no matter what you are feeling— even if it is ugly and dark—you are not alone. You can change the direction of your story. You can let the light in.

Push yourself. Push yourself to dream. Push yourself to love. Push yourself to love who you are for all the good and the bad. Life will get better. You are worthy just the way you are. Most importantly, we all are worthy of love.

Slowly and surely, each and every day now, my journey of recovery continues. Part of the process is to consciously remind myself that I am worthy of love and healing.

Healing takes a long time. But even the fact that I am able to share this story now and can look back to where I was with perspective and see a difference shows me how far I have already come. I can see that I am succeeding at learning how to tackle difficult transitions in my life, such as moving from my childhood home, changing my academic major again and again, and slowly rebuilding myself into the best possible version of who I can be—for the world, and more importantly, for myself.

In sharing my story with you, I have discovered a sense of purpose. I finally see a new light emerging, and feel that I am living up to the true meaning of my name.

You can do this too, I promise you.

Acknowledgments

To those who love me and whom I love, I sincerely apologize for any pain you have experienced because of my illness. My inability to show my love for you and the way I was acting while I was struggling were the result of chronic pain and self-hatred. I truly could not love anyone else before first feeling love for myself. Please know that I have come a long way in a short amount of time and I am feeling much better. I am starting to see myself as beautiful for all that I am.

I would like to acknowledge the following people who have been instrumental in my recovery and in the writing and publication of this book. Thank you:

- Mom and Dad: Your unconditional love and encouragement to follow my heart and do whatever I need in order to become the best version of myself.
- Mia, Declan, and Rory (Callie, Tillie, and Tiki, too): For being the best siblings in the world. I love you guys.
- Pam and Maiken: For being the strongest, most inspiring, and life changing women I have ever met.
- Diana, Stacey, and Dr. Borus: For being there as I took my first steps in recovery.
- Stephanie Gunning: For believing in me and my work. Your help has set me free to realize my dream of publishing this book.
- Lee Tilghman: For your blog "Lee from America" which helped me realize that I am not alone in this struggle. Your inner and outer beauty, creativity, and joy of living life have been a blessing for me to see.

- Big Brenda: For your daily emails, which have made me fall off my chair laughing. I truly value our vanilla ice cream with coffee and gossiping with you until godly hours about ALL the latest scandals!
- Grandma: For your sweet and gentle kindness. Your infinite love supporting me no matter what means so much to me. .
- Jack and Deborah: For your faith in me as a writer, and your constant affirmations of care and love.
- Brenda and Alex: For allowing me to be a part of your beautiful family.
- Paul and Liza: For being just a phone call away no matter what issue (or latest boy drama) I am having. I am so grateful for all of our NYC adventures.
- Professor Amy Morel l'Horset: For reading my book before anyone else truly wanted to. Your nutrition class gave me inspiration for my life. Your support and belief in who I am changed me.
- Professor Andrea Vazzana: For talking to me on the last day of class. Seeing your care and admiration for my story, and your belief in my work were powerful. Your class also changed my life and taught me that I CAN and I AM WORTHY of writing a book.
- Professor Cate Fallon: For sharing your wealth of knowledge on photography and creative imaging. This allowed me to harness the creativity needed to design my cover.
- Shanieka, Marni, and Jennifer: For being the greatest NYU advisors. I always know you have my best interest at heart. Thanks for unconditionally supporting my changing and evolving career.

- Doug, Heidi, and Coach Walsh: For seeing me as a leader and reminding me to be brave while doing whatever I need to care for myself.
- Mr. T, and Mr. Judge: For having faith in me as a musician, and for being people I will look up to for the rest of my life.
- The whole DYC pool staff: I am grateful to you for continually making me laugh within my worst moments, for accepting and respecting me and never questioning me about why I was suddenly not around. I am and will always be grateful for each of you.
- All the kids I have been lucky enough to help teach to swim: You made me believe in my ability to help others accomplish and learn new things. Thank you.
- Maggie, Maggie, Grace, Sarah, Sarah, Nikki, Annabelle, my childhood best friends: I will love and cherish all of you for my whole life no matter what.
- Ryan, Zina, Audrey, Madison, Grace, Rosa: Words cannot do any of you justice. I would not have made it back to NYU if it were not for your friendship.
- Shivali and Mike: I don't know if *hero* suffices as a strong enough word to describe the two of you. Your unconditional support helped me create a new beginning to my life at NYU. Shivali, you picked me up off of the floor . . . literally . . . I look up to you tremendously and always will. Mike, your genuine kindness through some of the hardest days of my sophomore year and your belief in my ability to succeed in chemistry have meant more to me than I think you probably could ever know.

Resources

To get updates on me and my writing, events, and endeavors, and to read my blog or get access to resources, visit my holistic health and wellness website: www.lucyquigley.com

For media inquiries or an invitation to speak to your group either in person or via webcam or phone, please contact me by email: lucyquigley@lucyquigley.com

Please follow me on the following social networks:
- **Instagram:** @lucyquigley11
- **Twitter:** @lucyquigley11
- **Facebook:** https://www.facebook.com/lucymquigley

PROFESSIONAL AND PEER RESOURCES

National Suicide Prevention Lifeline
A free 24-hour hotline for anyone in emotional distress.
Phone: 1-800-273-8255

In need of immediate medical attention? Call 911.

National Association of Anorexia Nervosa and Associated Disorders
Website: www.ANAD.org
Helpline: 1-630-577-1330 (M–F: 9:00–5:00 Central)

National Eating Disorders Association
Website: www.nationaleatingdisorders.org
Helpline: 1-800-931-2237 (M–F: 8:30–4:30 Eastern)

NEDA offers a free, confidential online screening to get a
baseline of symptoms and awareness to help you determine if
you or a loved one is at risk for an eating disorder.
http://screening.mentalhealthscreening.org/NEDA

**Walden Eating Disorder Treatment Centers
(Massachusetts)**
New England's leading program for treating eating disorders.
Website: www.waldeneatingdisorders.com
Phone: 1-781-647-6727

**Mirasol Eating Disorder Recovery Centers
(Arizona)**
Website: www.mirasol.net
Phone: 1-888-520-1700

Unsure about what to do or where to start? Go to your school
guidance counselor or health and wellness center to seek
advice and resources.

Overeaters Anonymous
A free twelve-step peer group with meetings in every state.
Website: www.oa.org

Index

ABOUT THE AUTHOR

Lucy Quigley currently attends New York University. She is planning to pursue a degree in nutrition to help others who are struggling with disordered eating like her.
Lucy grew up with a passion for writing and other arts. Writing runs in her veins, as her grandfather Martin S. Quigley was a veteran of the film and publishing industries, and had a nearly sixty-year-long career at Quigley Publishing Company. Lucy hopes to make him proud as his first grandchild to publish a book. She seeks to recreate and continue this beautiful legacy through the power of writing and telling stories.

CPSIA information can be obtained
at www.ICGtesting.com
Printed in the USA
LVOW11s1728170417
531098LV00002B/295/P